LEARN TO DRAW

Disney fairies

TinkerBell

Illustrated by The Disney Storybook Artists

Designed by Shelley Baugh • Project Editor: Rebecca J. Razo

Walter Foster

Year after year, the seasons come and go—with a little help from the fairies.

Every fairy starts out as a baby's first laugh, and this story is about one very special laugh. It traveled all the way from wintry London to the magical land of Pixie Hollow. There, the laugh touched down in the Pixie Dust Tree and became a fairy!

All around the new fairy, toadstools sprung up like pedestals. Fairies came forward and placed different objects on the toadstools—a drop of water, a flower, a tiny egg, and more—to help the new arrival find her talent.

The new fairy cautiously approached each object. At first, nothing happened, but when she passed by a small hammer, it began to glow brightly. The fairy Queen declared that the new fairy was a tinker—and a very powerful one! Her name was Tinker Bell.

Tinker Bell's first day was a busy one. First she met Clank and Bobble, two other tinkers, and Fairy Mary, the fairy in charge of the workshop in Tinkers' Nook. Later, she helped deliver tools to other fairies. Nature fairies needed the tools to bring spring to the mainland. The mainland was where the big people lived, and Tink thought it sounded wonderful. She couldn't wait to visit!

While Tinker Bell was out making deliveries with her new friends, she met Fawn, Rosetta, Iridessa, and Silvermist. They were nature fairies, and Tink liked them immediately. On the way back to Tinkers' Nook, Tink met Vidia, a fast-flying fairy. Vidia made it clear she didn't think much of the tinkers.

Tink was upset by what Vidia said about tinkers, and she flew away in a huff. As she passed a nearby beach, something caught her eye. She went to take a closer look and discovered many strange objects strewn about the sand. Fascinated, Tinker Bell gathered the objects in her arms and headed home.

Back at Tinkers' Nook, Tinker Bell showed off her treasures. Fairy Mary said they were junk—Lost Things—washed up from the mainland. She told Tink to get back to work, and Tink reluctantly put the Lost Things away in her workshop.

That night, Queen Clarion was to review the preparations for spring. Tink decided that this was her chance to prove herself, and she rushed to create several devices to make spring preparations easier. But when she tried to demonstrate how to use them, none of them worked. To top off Tink's disappointment, Queen Clarion told her that tinker fairies didn't even go to the mainland! Tinker Bell's efforts had been for nothing. She felt like she didn't matter at all.

But inspiration struck Tinker Bell a second time. She decided she would change her talent! She would become a nature fairy instead of a tinker, and she would go to the mainland after all. Tink tried to be a water fairy, a light fairy, and an animal fairy—but it was no use. Nothing went right and Tink felt worse than ever.

Tinker Bell went to the beach to be alone; there she found a broken music box. By the time her friends caught up with her, she had put it back together—and she'd enjoyed doing it. Tink's friends reminded her that she had a wonderful talent as a tinker. Perhaps this was what she was really meant to do! But tinkers didn't go to the mainland—and Tink still had her heart set on that.

Desperate, Tink asked Vidia for help. The spiteful fairy told Tink that if she could round up the Sprinting Thistles—dangerous weeds that left a path of destruction in their wake—it would prove she was a garden fairy, and then she could go to the mainland! Tink did her best, but the thistles wound up stampeding into Springtime Square. They trampled all the carefully organized springtime supplies and destroyed everything.

All the preparations for spring were ruined, and it was Tinker Bell's fault. Tink was about to leave Never Land forever, but she made one last visit to her workshop. She hated to admit it, but she did love to tinker—if only her inventions worked! Looking around her workshop, she had an idea. Tink gathered up the Lost Things she'd found on the beach and spread them out before her. She had work to do.

That night, Tink raced to Springtime Square with her new inventions. She promised everyone that the contraptions she made from Lost Things could put springtime together again in no time. And she was right! When the sun rose the next morning, the fairies were ready to bring spring to the world. "You did it, Tinker Bell," congratulated Queen Clarion.

Tink was happy—but she was even happier when Fairy Mary told her she could go to the mainland. Her job would be to return the music box she had fixed to its owner! And so, she joined all of her friends as they flew over the sea to the mainland for the change of seasons. Tinker Bell had finally found her place by staying true to herself.

Tools and Materials

The art fairies of Pixie Hollow use tiny, delicate twig-and-feather paintbrushes to paint the spots on ladybugs. But all you'll need for this book are normal, human-sized supplies. To begin, sketch your fairy with a regular pencil. You'll want to have a pencil sharpener and an eraser on hand as well. When you've drawn your fairies just the way you want them, you can bring them to life with a little color! Use crayons, felt-tip markers, watercolors, colored pencils, or even acrylic paints to color in your fairies.

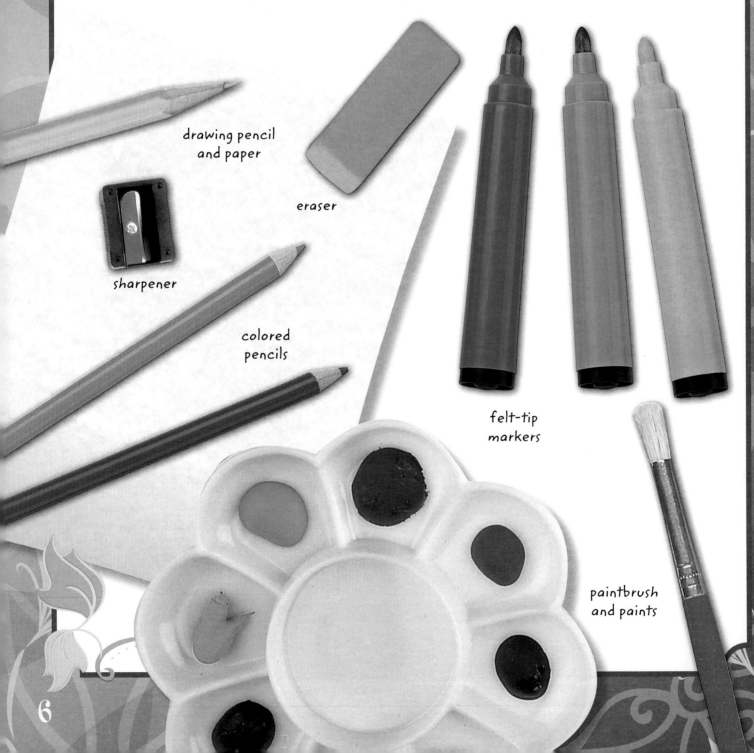

drawing pencil and paper

eraser

sharpener

colored pencils

felt-tip markers

paintbrush and paints

How to Use This Book

You don't need the skills of an art fairy to follow these simple steps!

Step 1

First draw the basic shapes using light lines that will be easy to erase.

Step 2

Each new step is shown in blue, so you'll know what to add next.

Step 3

Follow the blue lines to draw the details.

Step 4

Now darken the lines you want to keep, and erase the rest.

Step 5

Use fairy magic (or crayons or markers) to add color to your drawing!

Tinker Bell

This spirited tinker fairy is the latest arrival in Pixie Hollow. She shakes things up a bit but soon settles into her new home. Her specialty is inventing contraptions using human objects that wash up on the shores of Never Land. Tink has a big imagination—and an even bigger heart!

Step 1

Step 2

YES!
bun points up

NO!
bun not
too low

Tink's hair from
the back

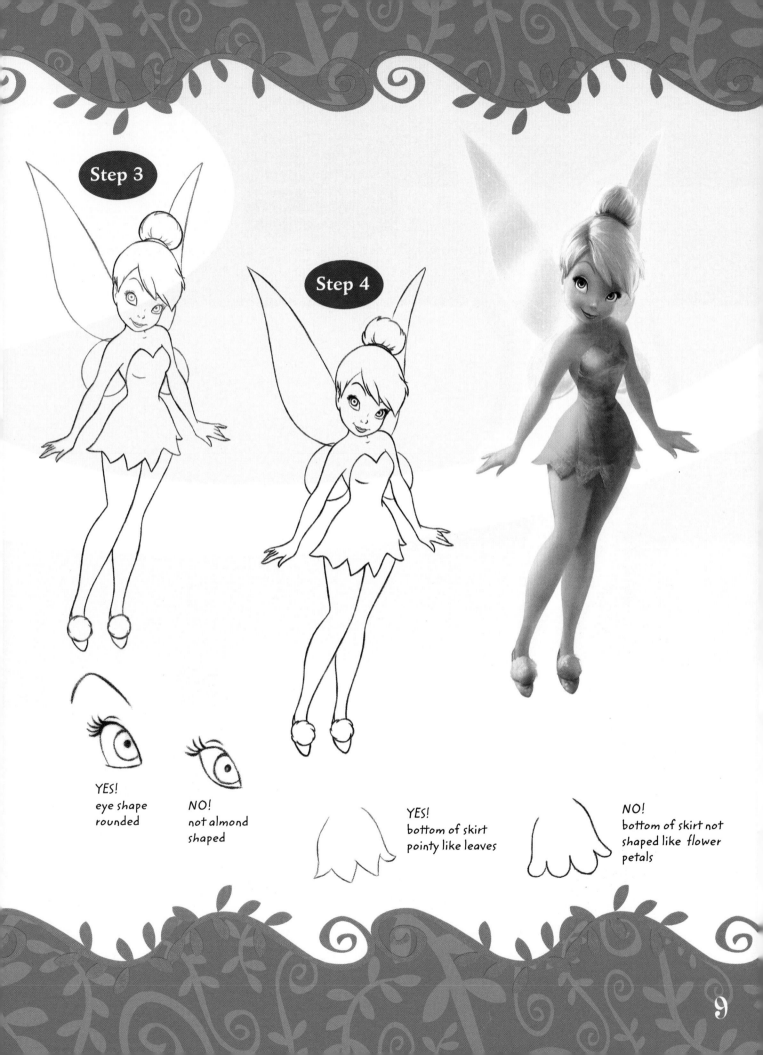

Step 3

Step 4

YES!
eye shape
rounded

NO!
not almond
shaped

YES!
bottom of skirt
pointy like leaves

NO!
bottom of skirt not
shaped like flower
petals

Fairy Mary

Fairy Mary is the stern, hardworking leader of the tinker fairies. She keeps everything running smoothly in Tinkers' Nook and takes great pride in her talent. She and Tink don't always see eye to eye, but they have great respect for each other.

Think of similarities to these Disney Characters

Nanny,
101 Dalmatians

Merryweather,
Sleeping Beauty

Mrs. Potts,
Beauty and
the Beast

Step 1

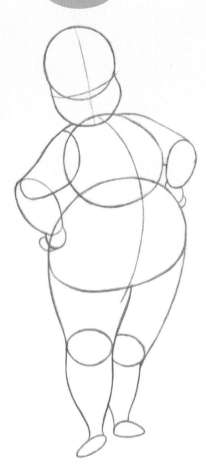

Step 2

Step 3

sometimes carries an abacus— a tool for counting

Step 4

round shapes create body structure

Silver Mist

Friendly and eager to please, the water fairy Silvermist has occasionally been described as "gushy." She's got a good heart, even if she does seem to change her mind every ten minutes!

YES!
hair is
long and
tapers

NO!
hair is
not cut
straight

strand of hair
falls in front of
one shoulder

Step 1

Step 2

Step 3

Step 4

Silvermist's dress is made
from lily petals

YES!
eyes set
at angle

NO!
eyes not
set on
straight
line

Rosetta

Rosetta, a garden fairy, has a quick wit and a ton of charm.
Beautiful and sensible, Rosetta sees right to the heart of every problem.

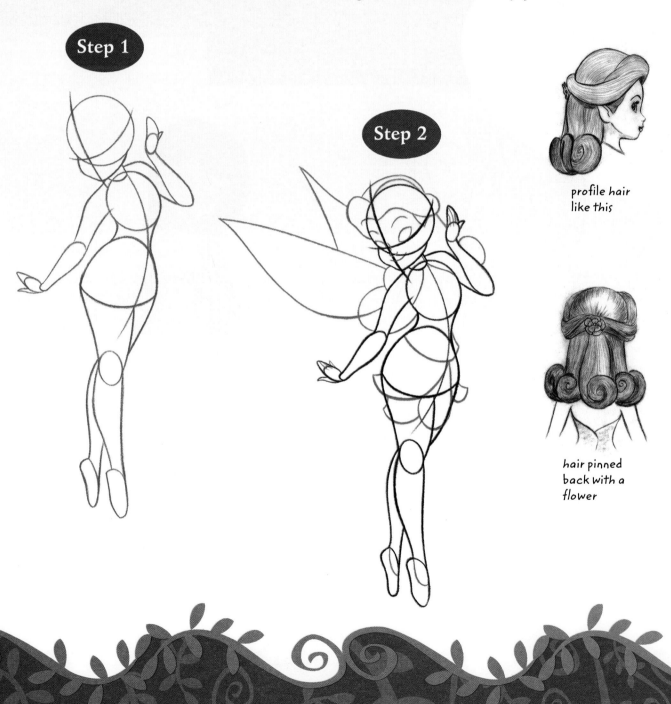

Step 1

Step 2

profile hair
like this

hair pinned
back with a
flower

Step 3

Step 4

YES!

NO!

Rosetta's dress is made from rose petals

Iridessa

Iridessa is a thoughtful fairy who likes to do everything exactly right, especially when it comes to her job. No other light fairy catches the last rays of sunlight with quite the same precision as Iridessa.

Step 1

Step 2

YES!
hair in
sections

NO!
hair not
smooth

YES!
slender chin,
full lips

NO!
cheeks not
too full

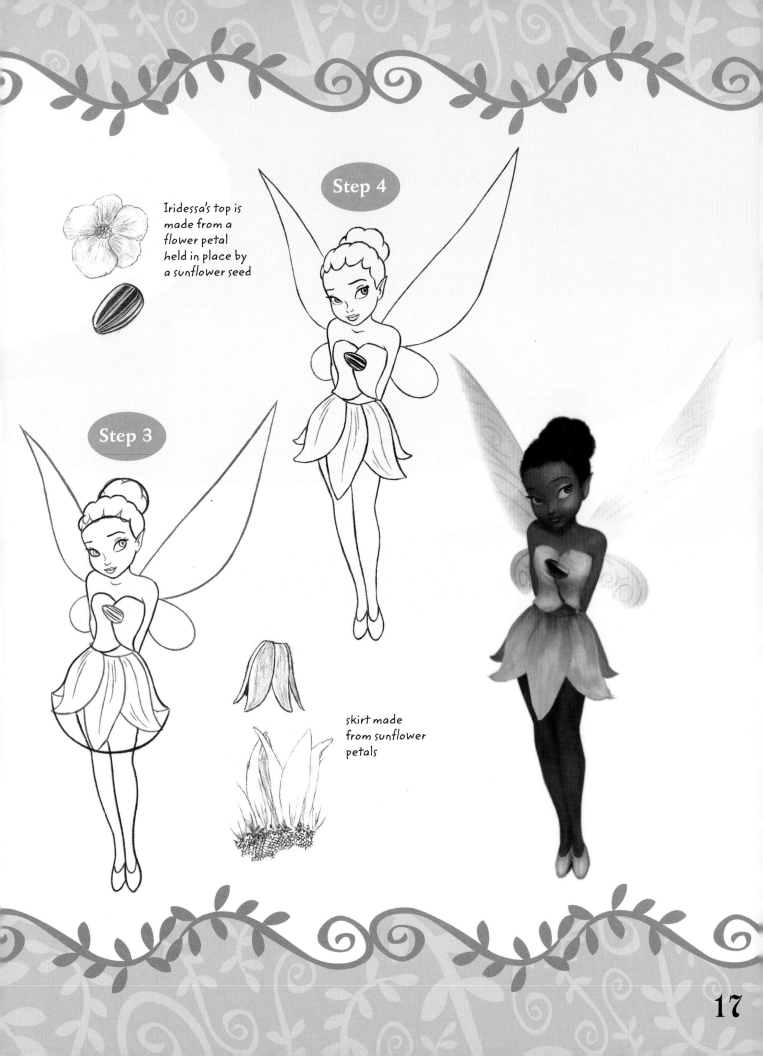

Iridessa's top is
made from a
flower petal
held in place by
a sunflower seed

Step 4

Step 3

skirt made
from sunflower
petals

Fawn

Fawn is the greatest prankster Pixie Hollow has ever known, but she's also the biggest softie. She loves the animals she cares for, and they love her.

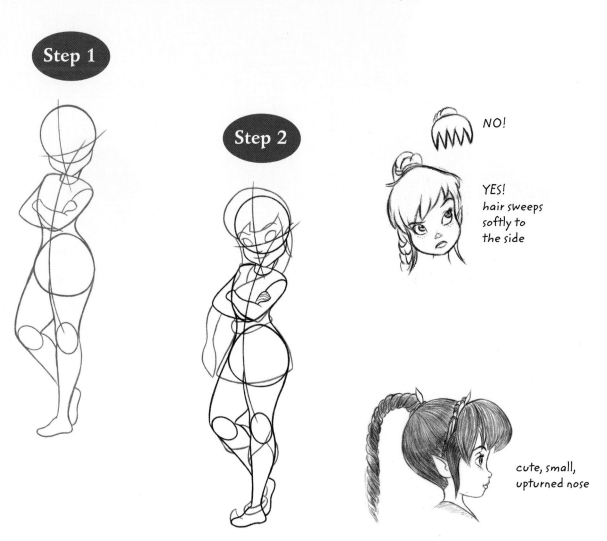

Step 1

Step 2

NO!

YES!
hair sweeps softly to the side

cute, small, upturned nose

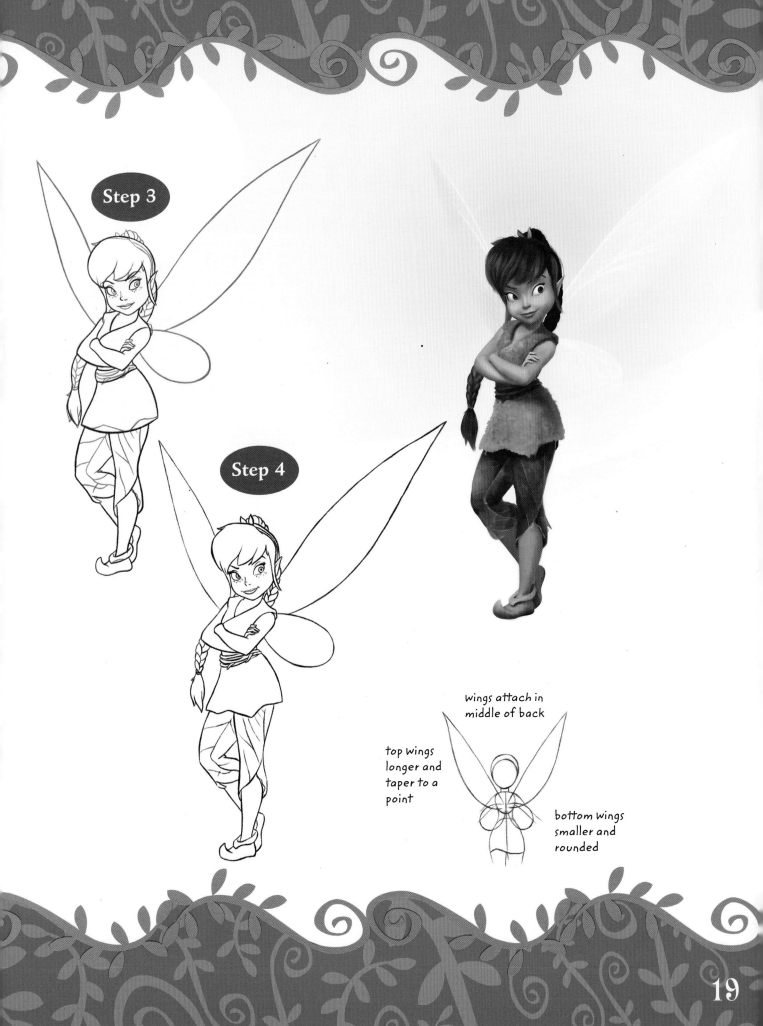

Step 3

Step 4

wings attach in
middle of back

top wings
longer and
taper to a
point

bottom wings
smaller and
rounded

Vidia

Spiteful Vidia loves being known for her talent and resents any competition—especially from Tinker Bell. But Vidia's schemes against Tink backfire, and the fast-flying fairy is left with the thankless job of rounding up the Sprinting Thistles.

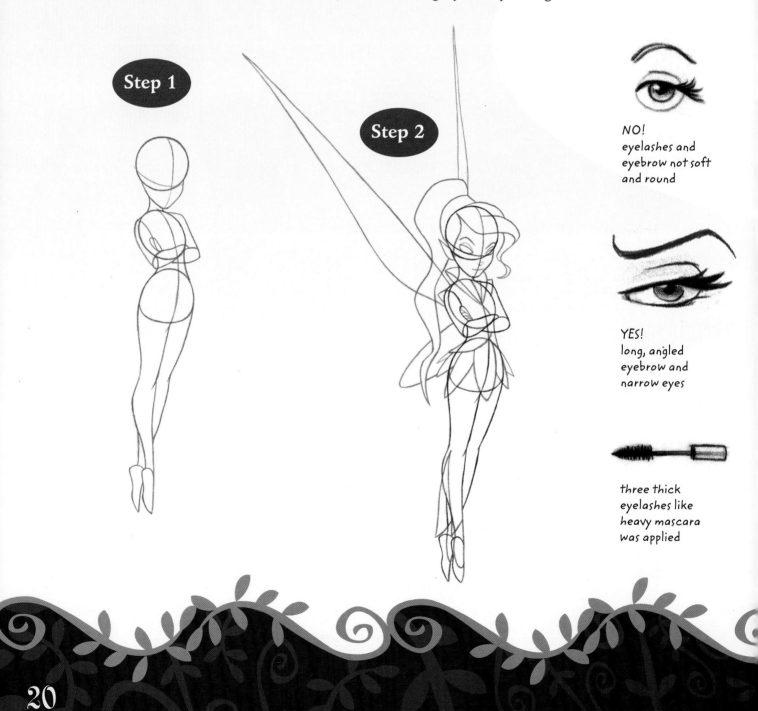

Step 1

Step 2

NO!
eyelashes and
eyebrow not soft
and round

YES!
long, angled
eyebrow and
narrow eyes

three thick
eyelashes like
heavy mascara
was applied

Step 3

Step 4

YES!
ponytail twists
and turns

NO!
ponytail not
straight

Queen Clarion

Queen Clarion is the wise ruler of the fairies. Her magic is so powerful that she sometimes travels in a mist of pure pixie dust.

Step 1

Step 2

Queen Clarion wears three different crowns for separate occasions

everyday crown

arrival crown

spring crown

Step 4

Step 3

Queen Clarion's wings are like a butterfly's

YES! eyes are almond shaped

NO! not too round

Clank

Clank and Bobble are the very best of friends. There's no trouble these two tinkers haven't gotten into! They really admire Tinker Bell for her talent and skill.

Step 1

Step 2

Clank puts cotton in his ears when he's working

Step 3

Clank
is shaped
like a fig

Step 4

wears a
tunic made
of a leaf

carries a jug
made from a
nutshell

Bobble

Bobble likes to hang out with his good friend Clank. These goofy pals love to fiddle, fix, craft, and create. Bobble's "glasses" are actually dewdrops set in blades of grass!

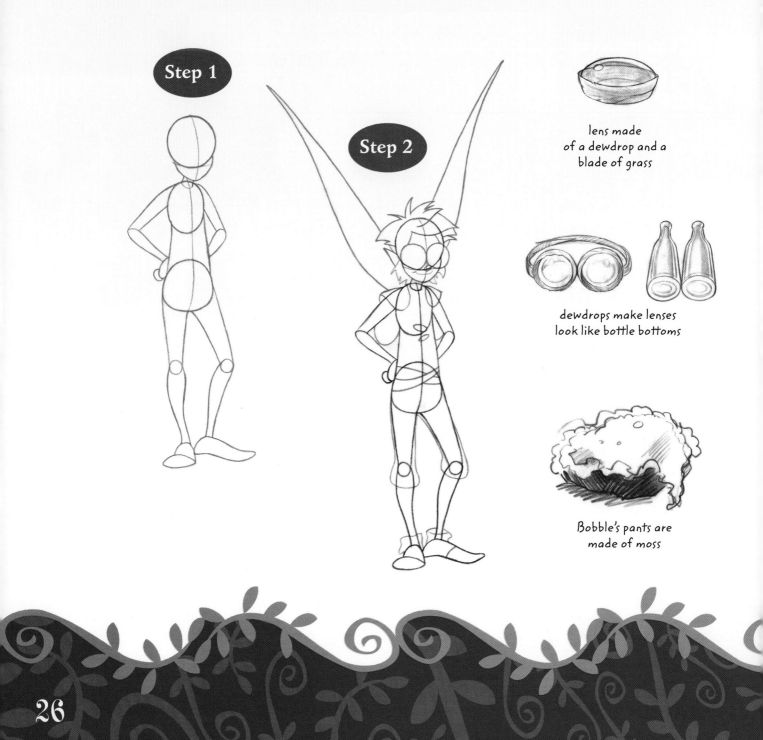

Step 1

Step 2

lens made of a dewdrop and a blade of grass

dewdrops make lenses look like bottle bottoms

Bobble's pants are made of moss

Step 3

Bobble is thin like a twig

Step 4

YES! hair thick and wavy on top; short in back

NO! hair not flat and long

Terence

Terence is a dust-keeper fairy and Tinker Bell's best friend. He knows how important each and every fairy talent is and takes great pride in the work he does for the fairies of Pixie Hollow.

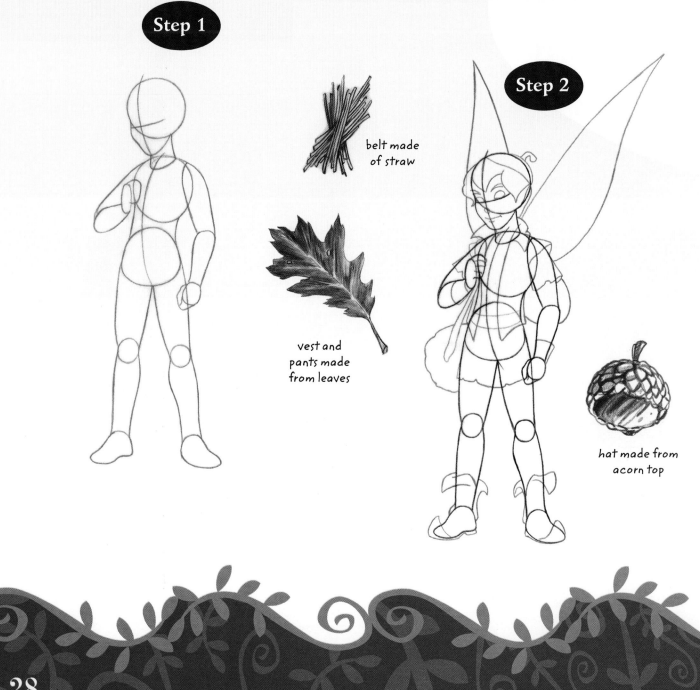

Step 1

Step 2

belt made of straw

vest and pants made from leaves

hat made from acorn top

Step 3

Step 4

dispenses daily
rations of pixie dust

shoulder bag
made from
walnut shell

Draw Your Own Fairy Scene

In enchanted Pixie Hollow, where the fairies of Never Land live, all four seasons exist at once. The snowflake fairies practice their arts in Winter Woods, while the fairies of Summer Glade sweeten peaches with pixie dust. And nearby, autumn and spring fairies are always busy as well. Tinker Bell's favorite view of Never Land is from high up in the air, where she can see every corner of her magical home.

Here's your chance to draw a scene from Pixie Hollow! First sketch an outline of your scene. Then add animals, plants, flowers, trees, or other fairy friends. Add color with crayons or markers. Be creative and have fun!

In Pixie Hollow, every day is full of magic.